W9-BNE-847

ADULT LEARNERS
SURVIVAL SKILLS

by **BILL BITTEL**
Illustrated by **JUDY BITTEL**

Robert E. Krieger Publishing Company
Malabar, Florida
1990

Original North American Edition 1990
(based on "I Hate to Study, A Book of Survival Skills for Adult Learners"
Produced in Australia 1987

Printed and Published by
ROBERT E. KRIEGER PUBLISHING COMPANY, INC.
KRIEGER DRIVE
MALABAR, FLORIDA 32950

Copyright ©1987 by William H. Bittel
Reprinted by Arrangement

Library of Congress Cataloging-in-Publication Data
Bittel, William H.
    Adult learners survival skills / by William H. Bittel :
illustrated by Judy Bittel.--Original North American ed.
        p. cm.
    Rev. ed. of: I hate to study / Bill Bittel. c1987.
    ISBN 0-89464-403-3 (alk. paper)
    1. Study, Method of. 2. Adult education. I. Bittel, William H.
I hate to study. II. Title.
LC5225.M47B58 1989
374'.13--dc20   89-33605
                                                    CIP

10   9   8   7   6   5   4   3   2

LC
5225
.M47
B58
1990

1974·0612

TABLE OF CONTENTS

This book is dedicated to the illustrator who worked with the author to turn academic jargon into plain English. When asked about this dedication, her only comment was, *It sounds a bit wordy to me!*

INTRODUCTION

Some adults, it is said, like to study. This book is not for them.

This book is for those who hate to study. It is for those who have learned through hard experience that some activities become no less painful through repetition: paying taxes, cleaning the house, washing and polishing the car.

The problem for most adults is that the goals they want to achieve often involve some kind of study. The days in which you could learn all you needed to know while you were young are gone. Recognizing this, you may have signed up for an evening class with good intentions and some enthusiasm. When you arrive on time the first night and look around the room, you see a group of highly intelligent and motivated people. The course description said "Introduction to ..." and it used words like "Designed for those with no knowledge of . . ." Casual conversation with the persons sitting on both sides of you has convinced you that they are both "experts" who have come for a re-fresher course.

When you turn for help to a book about study skills, it often begins with a statement, "You know that study can be one of the most satisfying pleasures you experience . . ." They can stop right there because in your experience study is plain hard work. When you perservere in reading the book, you often do not understand what you are supposed to do. Such books seem to have been written by experts for readers who are also experts.

They often contain too much information, such as how to conduct a computer search for information in the library, when your problem is understanding the first chapter in your textbook. What you want are some things you can do which will help you understand what you read, and enable you to be successful in your course.

This book offers you a series of simple, practical steps which you can take to improve your own study skills. The chapters cover the basic study skills of getting organized, reading, listening, writing and preparing for examinations. It is written in "plain English" and shows you how you can use your life experience when you study.

This book is the outcome of many years of talking to adults about their study skills and the problems they have encountered when returning to study. The ideas have not been tested by experts or subjected to some kind of computer analysis, but they have been used by many adults who have been successful in their study. You probably already know some of these things. If you do, this will boost your self-confidence.

The "expert" who sits next to you in class will not appear quite so smart the next time you talk to him or her.

You will know that this book has helped you when you enter your class or meet with a group of other students and realize that they are not super-human. They are just like you. They have varying degrees of ability, goals they want to achleve, problems which worry them and many different reasons for studying. Many of them probably felt inferior to you the first time they met you.

Unfortunately there are no magical solutions to problems. You will find ideas and practical suggestions in this book which you can use. You may also find some ideas which will give you a new insight into yourself and what you are doing. At the very least, you should find that there is someone who understands your concerns and problems. It is nice to know that you are not alone.

CHAPTER 1

ADULT LEARNERS, OR WHY DIDN'T I DO THIS YEARS AGO?

An adult learner is someone who looks just like you. They come in varying sizes, ages and conditions, but have one thing in common: they all hope that learning is not something done only by children in school. Their numbers have increased dramatically in recent years. Their habitats are schools, colleges, universities, libraries, workshops and any other place where learning takes place.

Some estimates say that as many as 80% of adults spend many hours each year learning something, either by themselves or with a group. The reason they do this is simple: they want something. For example, do you want to learn a new skill, change your job, earn more money, develop a hobby or learn more about yourself? These would be just a few of the many reasons why adults study. Their reasons are as numerous as the people who do it.

You selected this book because you want to learn, but you are not sure you can do it. Learning and study remind you only too well of school and Miss Ramrod. She was of indeterminate age, could see in all directions at once and

had psychic powers. She always knew when you did not know the answer. The only good days were the ones when she was absent, and those were rare as she had a constitution of iron.

Still there is something you want, a goal you want to achieve. To get it you will have to make some effort. Your goal may be concrete like buying a new car or abstract like being happy. Start by putting aside your memories of Miss Ramrod.[1]

---

[1] Some readers may have had a Mr. or Mrs. or Ms. Ramrod. Sex and marital status made no difference. You know who we mean if you were in such a class. We will refer to her/him as "The Ramrod" from now on.

Now think about where you are and where you want to go. Ask yourself, "What do I want?" Make a list of ten things which, if you had them, would make a big difference in your life. Don't list things like "winning a million dollars", but do list things which you could do. When you complete your list, number the items in their order of importance.

Now look at your list. What does it tell you

about yourself? Show your list to a close friend and ask what they think. The point of making the list is to gain a clearer picture of your ambitions and goals. Knowing what you want is an important step in building your own self-confidence so you can achieve your goals.

The second step is to think about what you can do now. There must be some things that you can do or you would not think about study and you would not read this book. This time make two lists. At the top of one put "Things I do well", and at the top of the other put "Things I should improve." Think first about what you can do and then about improving.

Where are you now? You have started thinking about study skills and you are using suggestions from this book. You are working without The Ramrod looking at you in that "meaningful" way. You are applying general principles of learning to your life.

This is important because all "How to Study" books talk about study skills in general ways. You are unique. You have specific interests and needs. Before this book can help you, you have to "translate" its general ideas into things you can and will do.

You will change what you do when you can see that it will help. The only way to find out if it will help is to try it. New methods may not at first work as well as your old method. But give the new idea some time. When it works, the result will be obvious.

If you listed all the things you do when you study, they would be a summary of your learning style. Just as you can see that a person dresses with style, you can see their learning style by observing how they learn.

Learning styles are affected by the environment, emotions, people and personal preferences. The environment includes things like location, temperature, light, etc. For example, do you like to work in a quiet room or do you like music playing in the background or other people in the room? What is the room temperature which you call comfortable? Do you like to study at home, on the beach, in a library or soaring in a hot air balloon?

The emotional element of your learning style includes things like motivation (how much you want to do it), and your persistence (how long you work at it). Some people prefer to attend classes and others prefer to study on their own. Do you like a textbook which gives you the facts or do you want to read several books to find out for yourself? All these things involve feelings and make a difference in your learning.

The social element involves other people. The Ramrod was an important part of the social environment of your school, but you called her/him something else. Other people influence how and what we learn. Do you enjoy being in class with other students? What kind of a teacher do you prefer? Do you worry when other people get better results than you do in tests and assignments? These are examples of social influences on your learning.

The physical elements of your learning style involve how you learn. Can you fix anything around the house, or do you have five thumbs when it comes to repair jobs? Some people learn

by hearing, others by doing, some by seeing and some by a combination of these. Do you sit quietly when you study, or do you like to move around? Do you learn best in the morning, afternoon or evening? Some people eat, chew gum, drink coffee and do other things.

All these things make up your personal learning style. Think about what you do. Knowing more about your own preferences will help you make better use of your time.

TAKING A FIRST STEP

There is an old Chinese proverb which says, "The longest journey begins with a single step." Getting started is often difficult when you study. There are so many reasons for doing it later.

You can't neglect your work because you like to eat regularly and live indoors, and when you do have a free moment, you are tired. At home there is always something that should be done or the phone rings or there is some crisis. If you work and run a home, the problems seem to treble.

By now you are nodding your head and thinking, "I know what he means. . ." There are problems, but ask yourself a couple of questions: "Where do I want to be a year from now?"

"What is the first small step I can take right now to get moving?" Your first step was to read this book. What is your second? What can you do today to work toward your goal? Do you have a book to read? You cannot read the whole book, but you can read the first chapter today. Read another chapter tomorrow and so on until you finish the book.

O.K. you have started, but what about that other saying about old dogs and new tricks? Adults often ask, "Am I too old to learn?" The answer is simple. If you are still alive, you are not too old.

Adults can and do learn new things when the skills and knowledge are something they want. When you see that it is relevant to your needs and interests, you will learn.

You also work best when you work at your own pace. Adults will sacrifice speed for accuracy. They want to know the why and how of things. It may take you slightly longer to learn, but you can do it.

FRIENDS AND OTHER DISTRACTIONS

Friends and family come in varying shapes and sizes. Some are pleased when they learn that you want to study, and some say, "Why do you want to do that?" This implies that there is something wrong with you.

What this person is really saying is, "You are going back to study and I am not. I feel inferior to you." They feel threatened by you. You are doing something and they are not.

Others may urge or demand that you do something else. They say it is "terrific" that you are studying, but would you do something for them instead? It may be help with homework, cooking, extra work at the office, attend a committee meeting or something else.

The trouble is you feel guilty. You used to

do those things and now you are doing what you want to do. Look for a way to do both if necessary. Explain to the other person why you have to study and suggest another time for their job. Perhaps someone else can do it for you. Other family members can wash the dishes and a subordinate can gain valuable experience attending that committee meeting.

Now you are ready to study and you start. After about ten to fifteen minutes you find your mind is wandering. You start thinking about other things that need doing. Perhaps your friend was right after all - old dogs, you know.

You're normal. It is just that you have a short concentration span. When we enjoy something, we do it for a long time. When it is hard, we work for a shorter time. Studying and learning can be hard work. So if you find your mind wandering, take a short coffee break. After five minutes, come back to your work.

If you find you are drinking too much coffee, you can extend your concentration span. Find out how long you work. Let's say it is fifteen minutes. For the next couple of days, work in fifteen minute intervals with five minute breaks.

Once you do this as a routine, add five minutes to your study time. Now you are working for twenty minutes before you take a break. Of course, you probably look at your watch several times during that last five minutes. But keep going, work at it until twenty minutes becomes your new routine.

When it does, you can add an additional five minutes to it if you wish. There is no ideal amount of time you should study. Take a break when you need one and at least once an hour.

THE LAST WORD

Now you are thinking about what you want and how you will get it. You have learned something about your personal learning style and how small steps will help you achieve your goal. Focus on what you can do today and this week. You are older, but you are smarter too! You can do it if you want to do it.

CHAPTER 2

YOU DON'T LIKE TO
READ EITHER?

So you don't like to read? Some adults will do anything to avoid reading: cut the grass, wash the dog, or even take their mother-in-law out shopping.

While there is no magic formula, the ideas in this chapter have helped people in the past, who like you, were turning to study. People have been known to graduate from bubble gum wrappers to comic books in no time at all using these ideas.

When reading a difficult book, what do you do? Tear your hair out? Throw the book across the room? Swear at the dog? These methods may make you feel better, but they don't overcome your problem.

What happens when you read? Do you find books difficult to understand? Perhaps it isn't you. The book may use jargon or be hard to understand. What you want is a way to understand what you read. Consider the following statements about reading habits:

True or False?

1. If it is difficult, read it slowly.
2. You will understand more by re-reading parts of sentences.
3. Reading aloud will help you understand.
4. If you read faster, you will understand more.

Now look to the bottom of the this page and check your answers.

Did you get one or more wrong? Most people do. Some of our reading habits, like some other habits, are not really good for us.

Let's talk about reading habits. It might seem funny that reading slowly doesn't help. If you want to improve your tennis or golf, you slow

Answers to statements about reading habits:
1. False 2. False 3. False 4. True

down your swing. What' s wrong with slowing down when you read? When you learned to read, you read slowly because you were learning that those funny marks on the page related to real people and things.

Today you know what the words mean. The problem is finding out what some authors want to say by using those words. Here is an example:

"In sum, far from being a source of fully elaborated 'innate ideas', the maturation of the nervous system can do no more than determine the totality of the possibilities and impossibilities at a given stage. A particular social environment remains indispensable for the realization of these possibilities."[1]

[1]Inhelder, B. & Piaget, J., The Growth of Logical Thinking. London: Routledge & Kegan Paul, 1958, 337.

This is an overload of information and reading slowly does not change that. You are left to figure out what it means because you have to complete the assignment by Friday!

Will it help to look up the words in the dictionary? No. You know what the words mean, but you don't understand what the authors want to tell you by using those words.

Dictionaries give us general meanings of words. Authors use words to say something specific.

For example, "John is short for a profes-

sional basketball player" when he is 6'2", means something very different from "John is short for an adult Australian" when he is 4'8". The meaning of "short" changes depending on how it's used.

Another habit is reading aloud. You may have read aloud in The Ramrod's class because you had to. Now it just slows you down. You probably know one or two "fast talkers", but even they only talk at about 175 words per minute. An average reader can read at twice that speed. Fast talkers become slow, inefficient readers when they read aloud.

Your brain works quickly when you read, processing words and ideas at high speed. When you slow down, your brain often says to itself, "This is boring. Let's think about . . ." Your eyes may go on reading, but your brain will find something more interesting to think about.

O.K. How do you stop your brain daydreaming when you want to read? More to the point, how do you get information from books which confuse you?

LET'S LOOK AT READING TO LEARN

Reading to learn is not the same as reading for fun. For example if you read a detective novel, you don't read the last chapter first. The last chapter tells you "who dunnit". When you read to learn, you want the whole picture which includes "who dunnit", so read the last chapter first. If you are only reading one chapter in the book, read the conclusion first.

This method gives you a "preview" of the chapter or book. It's like watching T.V. where you see previews which show you the exciting parts of new programs. They give you some idea of what future programs are about. In reading, a preview gives you the main ideas in a book or chapter.

Here is a simple way to preview a chapter: first, read the introductory paragraph; then read only the first sentence of each following paragraph; finally, read the last paragraph.

This will give you an idea of what is in the chapter. Authors often put their major idea in the first sentence of a paragraph and you have now read all these first sentences. It only took you a few minutes. Now think about what you have read and ask yourself a question:

"What are the important points, the big ideas?"

Instead of feeling confused by the words, you are thinking about what they mean. You are relating major ideas to what you already know.

Now take a deep breath and start again! Read the whole chapter from beginning to end. Read at a speed which keeps you going. Don't re-read difficult parts and don't read aloud. If something is not clear, keep going. You may find an example further down the page which will explain the difficult part.

Be positive and don't be discouraged. You already know some of the ideas from your preview. Now you are reading to understand more about these major points. Help your understanding and concentration by asking these questions as you read:

1.   How do the important points fit in with
        what I already know?

2.   How am I going to use this information?

Now you are focusing on the meaning of what you read. You are less likely to dream of greener pastures like your five o'clock cocktail or what is for dinner. You are concentrating efficiently, but there may still be points which are not clear. This is why the third step, "reviewing", is important.

When you review a chapter, re-read the parts you thought were important. Were some parts not clear? It's just like the preview except that you select what you want to re-read. Sometimes it may be a whole chapter. For example, a Shakesperian play is written in old English which is hard to understand. It helps to read the play more than once. But only do this when there is a good reason for doing it.

These methods may not reduce mountains to mole hills, but they give you a way to understand what you read. As your understanding improves, you will enjoy reading more. You may find that you read more too.

This system assumes that you read silently. What can you do if you read aloud?

It sounds crazy, but place a pencil between your lips without touching it with your teeth. Now read.

If the pencil stays in place, you are O.K. You read silently. If it drops out, you need to practice reading with a pencil until you do not lose it. At this stage you are probably rolling around the floor with laughter!

You may look funny reading like this, but you will learn to read silently. Practice this method in private because if you have to stop frequently to explain to friends and strangers why you are reading with a pencil held between your lips, you may never stop talking.

WHAT ABOUT REMEMBERING?

You are reading and understanding more. Great! But do you ever read and understand something only to find that you cannot remember it a few minutes later? What went wrong? You read it, but your attention wandered. Perhaps you noticed an attractive person sitting near you, or some problem was bothering you.

Why do we remember some things we read and forget others? You remember your own name because it's important to you. We remember things which are important to us and often forget things which are not.

If you meet someone and you want to remember their name, you may repeat the person's name several times to yourself. Repetition helps you remember. Advertising uses repetition very successfully. For example, many people remember the Coke slogan because they see and hear it frequently. You probably never intended to remember it, but you do. So one way to remember is to repeat things.

Another way is to link something new to what you already know. When you read, if you relate new facts and ideas to things you know, this will help you remember them. Look for a connection, a way in which the new idea is related to the old. How are they similar and how different? Seeing similarities and differences will help you remember.

Suppose you want to remember a series of ideas or facts? This time you need to form a chain of connections. Take the first idea or fact and compare it to the second. How are they related to each other? Is there some logical connection between them? For example, you put the key in the ignition before you start your car. "Key - ignition - start" is a chain. Find something about the first item which will lead you to the second. This becomes the first link in your chain. Now repeat the process for the second and third ideas, and so on.

These are three simple methods which will help you remember what you read. They work when you have a purpose for remembering and when the information is going to help you in some way.

Making notes when you read also helps you remember. If the book belongs to you, make your notes in the margin or underline important points. However, don't write in library books because librarians become hostile when they discover your "improvements".

Read the chapter BEFORE you make notes. Then your notes are a summary of what you think is important. When you write down the important points, be brief. Don't re-write the

whole chapter, but do put the notes in your own words whenever possible. When you can do this, you really understand what you have read.

If you have difficulty "translating" the author's words into plain English, discuss the chapter with a friend. Explain what you think it means and have the other person ask you questions about it. You will have to explain the ideas and facts simply before your friend can understand them.

But there are times when the author's words are the best ones to express the ideas. For example, the quotation "The peasants voted with their feet" is brief and explicit. If you know what it means, the simplest way is to write it this way in your notes.

When you use the author' s words, put them in quotation marks ("), and put the page number at the end of the quotation. Write the author's name, title of the book and publication details at the top of your page. Publication details are where the book was published, who published it and the date it was published. Later if you want to use the quotation, you know where you found it.

You will also avoid problems when you use the quotation in an essay or report. Teachers are very "narrow minded" when students include sentences taken directly from books without using quotation marks. They may, quite un-fairly, accuse you of copying or cheating. You may be innocent, but they have had too many experiences with students who were not. They have even been known to spend hours in the library looking for the exact book to be used in evidence against you!

THE LAST WORD

Following these suggestions will help you understand what you read. Reading to learn is not the same as reading for enjoyment. When you read to learn, start with a preview which will give you a basic outline of the important points. Next read the chapter asking yourself questions which help you understand it. Think about how you will use the information and review the chapter to clarify important points. Help yourself remember by relating new ideas to what you already know. When you take notes, put the ideas into your own words. Reading and making notes are like other study skills. When you use an effective method, you improve with practice.

CHAPTER 3

LISTENING IS MORE THAN JUST BEING THERE

Listening is one study skill you have. You have listened to others talk for years. Other people may have trouble saying what they mean. In fact life would be a lot simpler if people would learn to say what they mean in plain English.

When you were in the Ramrod's class, there were times when you listened, but didn't understand what you heard. You used to look out the window thinking of where you would rather be.

When you study it's not easy to concentrate on what is being said. You may be tired if the class meets after work. There may be other things you should be doing, or you may have a problem. But you are there because you want to learn. Since you are spending one of your most valuable assets, time, you want value in return.

Let's begin by talking about what you do before you listen. When you enter the room, do you look around to see if you know anyone to talk to? When you talk to others, you talk about what you have been doing, mutual friends or common interests. Occasionally you talk about why you are there and what you hope to learn.

Since you are there to learn, you can get ready to listen by spending a few minutes thinking about what you have learned up to this point. How is it related to your work, your interests and needs? How will you use the information when the course is completed? If you had a chapter to read or an assignment, review what you did. Also read over your notes from the previous class. This will remind you of what was said.

Doing these things prepares you to listen. Sit where you can see and hear. Be ready to take notes. These things take only a few minutes, but they help.

When the class begins, pay attention. Listen actively. This involves more than letting the words flow around you as if you were in a pool. As you listen, ask yourself questions. Does what is being said agree, disagree, clarify or do what to the facts and opinions you already have? The kind of questions you ask depends upon the type of subject it is. In mathematics class, you want to be sure you understand the techniques for solving problems.   In a history class, you should ask if there is a different opinion or inter- pretation which you should consider. Active lis- tening means you ask questions.

At this point you may say, "Wait a minute! How can I listen and ask myself questions at the same time?"

It's easy. Even a fast talker is slow in comparison to your ability to listen. Your brain can process hundreds, even thousands, of words per minute. You can listen and think about what you hear at the same time.

REACTING WHILE LISTENING

When you think about what is said, you need to be careful not to reject ideas and theo- ries which conflict with what you know and be- lieve. As an adult you have an advantage be- cause your life experience is valuable. You have a lot of general knowledge, but you must keep an open mind to new information.   This is not easy and some adults stop listening when they hear something they do not agree with or like.

An example will illustrate the dangers of a closed mind. Mrs. "X", who had raised two children, enrolled in a class about child development. She wanted to be a teacher. But the Lecturer could not tell her anything about how children developed because "She was a mother and she knew". She rejected any fact, theory or opinion which questioned or challenged how she had raised her children, and she had a lot to challenge! She interpreted what the Lecturer said as a personal criticism. After six weeks she quit the class and finally gave up the idea of becoming a teacher. In retrospect, the Lecturer described Mrs. "X" as having a mind like cement: mixed up and permanently set.

Adults like Mrs. "X" are foolish. When you go to class, you want to learn and this means change. You may have to revise some of your opinions and discard some old knowledge because it is obsolete. When you hear something which challenges what you think, ask yourself, "What is the evidence for that theory? Is there an alternative?"

When you listen, focus on the message and not on the speaker. Remember your purpose. You want to understand so you can do the work. You also should focus on what you enjoy while still doing the work necessary to pass.

Listen for the main ideas and facts, separating them from things which illustrate or clarify. Take notes summarizing what has been said in your own words . List the major points and under them give the facts, details and examples. If you miss something, don't worry but keep listening. You can always ask a question at the end or you can look up the point for yourself.

Asking the teaohor questions and participating in discussions is another way of listening

actively. Not every teacher encourages questions, but if they do, ask. Don't worry whether you are asking an "intelligent" question as there will be several other people who wanted to ask the same question, but were afraid to do so.

Asking questions and discussing issues is not the same as challenging the Lecturer. This can be fun for those involved, but is usually frustrating for non-participants. You rarely learn anything when you argue because you only listen to be able to refute what is said. If you are there to learn, you want to understand what the other person has said. You do not learn by rejecting what you do not understand. Only question when you really want to know.

A different sort of problem is listening to someone who is dull or boring. As an adult learner you need to be tolerant. Academics are not always as polished as speakers on T.V. and it is hard for academics to compete! Try to suspend your judgment when you listen. The speaker may have habits like scratching his nose or pacing up and down, but you are there because the Lecturer knows something which you want to learn. You will learn more if you are tolerant.

The final stage of listening occurs after the class has ended. How can you listen if there is no class? It's easy. You can review what was said by thinking about it while reading your notes. You can review both what you heard and saw in this way. In about five minutes you can "see" and "hear" what occurred in class. The speed at which your brain works enables you to make this quick review.

You can make corrections and additions to your notes as well as thinking about connections between ideas. You can relate new information to what you already know.

If you review your notes within 24 hours of the class, you will remember most of what was

said and what happened. If you wait 48 hours, you will remember about half the material. The longer you wait to review, the less you will remember.

It's often an effort to review your notes. You get home and you are tired. There are lots of other things you should do. Remind yourself that by reviewing within 24 hours, you will save yourself time later because you will not have to re-learn this information. You will remember it.

GETTING IT ON PAPER

Before you can review your notes, you have to make them. You will not remember enough of what was said by just listening. So what is a good way to take notes?

Start by writing the date and subject at the top of the page. This way you can keep track of them. Write as legibly as you can because it is embarrassing not being able to read your own handwriting.

Listen for the first major point, fact or idea. Briefly write it down in your own words. Perhaps give it a number. Whenever possible "translate" the Lecturer's words into your own because the information will mean more to you. Of course, if you know what the words mean and they are brief and to the point, write down what is said. You can write sub-points, examples, illustrations, etc. under the major point.

Don't write everything that is said. Adults sometimes take too many notes because they worry that they will miss something important. Through practice you will learn what is and is not important.

Developing your own set of abbreviations will help you take notes. You are familiar with symbols like "&, @, +". You can create your own: C19 for nineteenth century; initials instead of names, GW instead of George Washington; p instead of probability when a word is used frequently. Just be sure you do not use the same symbol for more than one thing.

Writing your own notes using abbreviations is better than tape recording the whole class. While some students do this, it is a waste of valuable time. It takes as much time to listen to the tape as you spent in class. You can save time by reviewing with your notes, and use the extra time to read, solve problems, work on assignments, etc.

Another time waster is re-writing notes. If you want to memorize information, writing it again will help. But re-copying notes so they are "neat" is "busy work". Being busy is not the same as learning. As long as you can understand them, they will do the job. If you cannot understand them, re-write this set, and be sure to write more clearly in the next class.

THE LAST WORD

Listening is something you can do. When you listen ask yourself what you want to know. Focus on the content and not on how the message is presented. Listen for the important points, the big ideas, and separate them from the supporting examples, illustrations, details, etc. Make

an effort to ignore distractions. Ask yourself questions to maintain your interest. If something is not clear, ask for an explanation. If you take notes and review them within 24 hours, you will understand and remember most of what was said.

CHAPTER 4

WRITING OR HOW WOULD YOU PUT THAT?

"I know what I want to say, but I can't write it." Does that sound familiar? A lot of adults think that they cannot write. But you can learn to write if you want to.

Some only enrol in courses where writing is not required, and some get others to do their writing for them. There is a better way - learn to write. Decide you want to learn. Next practice writing since that is the way you learned to do most things. Finally learn from your successes and mistakes.

These are the easy, initial steps you can take to change the way you feel about writing. When we are good at something, we like to do it. Perhaps you are a "practical person", one who is good at "doing" things. That's good because writing is a practical skill. Remember when you were a child and you learned how to tie your shoe laces? It's not easy to learn that. Watch a child doing it for the first time. There are no "born writers" any more than there are "born shoe lace tiers". You learn both through practice.

Before you can write, you need something to write about. If you are writing about a novel, play or scientific experiment, you must read the novel or play or complete the experiment. This work is the background for your writing. It will become a source of ideas, even inspiration with a bit of luck.

Here you are, having made up your mind to write. Your paper, pen, books and notes are on your desk. There is only one thing missing: you can't think of a single good idea! Perhaps you should start tomorrow?

If you wait until you think of a "good idea", you may wait a very long time!

You want to write so make a list. You can do that. When you go to the supermarket, you make a list. You can use the same method in writing. A list does two things for you:

starts you writing instead of thinking about it; gives you a framework of facts and ideas.

Put everything that occurs to you on your list. When you run out of ideas, review your list. Which items look good? Which ones go together? Can you think of something to add? Cross out and change things as necessary.

CUBING OR MOVE OVER PICASSO

When you look at your list, it looks like a list. It is not your essay or report yet. What do you do next? This is when you use "cubing". "Cubing" is asking the following questions about the items on your list:

WHO? WHAT? WHERE? WHEN? WHY? HOW?

Ask each question about every item on your list and write down the answer. You may not get an answer every time, but your list will grow as you add information, facts, ideas, opinions, etc. When you have finished, you can start again asking the same questions about your answers.

Let's consider a practical example to illustrate the cubing technique. You are studying European history and have been reading about Germany after World War I. Your essay topic is, "How Hitler came to power", and you have an "information overload". Use cubing to get started.

WHO listened to Hilter and gave him support?
WHAT made Hilter into a successful politician?
WHERE did Hilter get money for his party?
WHEN did things go right and wrong for him?
WHY did people vote for his party?
HOW did he become important?

As you answer these questions, you organize what you know from your reading and develop points to include when you write. To continue the example, you might get the following answers to your questions.

WHO	There were lots of umemployed and ex-soldiers who listened to and supported him.
WHAT	People were fascinated when he spoke - one time they waited for hours standing in the rain just to hear him.
WHERE	Money came at first from individuals, later from big business.
WHEN	Bavaria was a mistake - the treason trail a triumph.
WHY	He offered hope in the future and solutions to problems.
HOW	He spoke in almost every town and city in Germany

These answers include facts and opinions from your reading. They give you a framework for your writing. Now you are ready to develop an outline of what you want to say.

"What's an outline and how do I write one?" It's a skeleton of your essay. The list you made was a brief outline. Look at your list again and find the things which are important, the big ideas. They are the ones to write about. An essay of average length may have five or six big ideas. A shorter essay will have fewer and a longer one will have more. Give each big idea a number.

Take the first one and read through your notes and books looking for things which relate to it. You want facts, opinions, details, etc., anything which will help you write about that point. When you find something, put a number 1 next to the item. Do this for each major point. When you finish, you will know which parts of your notes relate to your major points.

Next write each major point at the top of a separate page. Now make a brief summary on that page of the material in your notes which relates to that major point. When you do this for each item, you will have an outline of what you want to say.

Now you can turn your outline into paragraphs and it will start to look like an essay or report. Pick out a "topic sentence" around which you can build your paragraph. You will remember that a "topic sentence" is the big idea in the paragraph. You have the big ideas in your outline and now you are going to write about them.

For example, in your outline in response to the WHEN question, you wrote: "Bavaria was a mistake - the treason trial a triumph." You might write as your topic sentence, "In 1923 Hitler made a mistake in Bavaria." You know it was a mistake because he tried to overthrow the state government and failed.

The rest of that paragraph will explain why it was a mistake. You might continue, "Hitler expected the German Army to support him since the World War I hero, General Ludendorff, was with him. But the Army supported the government. "

Write enough to explain your major point. Check what you write against the topic sentence, asking, "How does this explain, clarify or support my topic sentence?" As long as it does, it belongs in the paragraph. If it doesn't support the topic sentence, take it out. A topic sentence paragraph is a group of sentences which talk about your major point.

A second type of paragraph is called a "function paragraph". This type introduces what you want to say, tells the reader how to interpret something, keeps interest alive or gains attention. The following example is a function paragraph used to gain the reader's attention.

"The ghost that got into our house on the night of November 17, 1915, raised such a hullaballoo of misunderstanding that I am sorry I didn't just let it keep on walking, and go to bed. Its advent caused my mother to throw a shoe through a window of the house next door and ended up with my grandfather shooting a patrolman."[1]

When you read this paragraph, you want

---

[1]Thurber, J., 'The night the ghost got in.' THE THURBER CARNIVAL. London: Hamilton, 1945

to know what happened. You may not be able to write like Thurber, but you can arouse your reader's interest with your introductory paragraph.

Essays and reports need an introduction, a middle and a conclusion. Cubing develops your ideas into paragraphs for the middle of your essay. The introduction is a function paragraph which introduces what you want to say. It tells the reader briefly what the essay is about, and the direction it will take. The conclusion is your brief summary at the end to remind the reader of what you have said. Each chapter in this book has an introductory paragraph and a conclusion.

FINISHING TOUCHES

Now for the bad news. Having written your essay, you should re-write it. Just when you thought all your problems were over too!

Re-writing is important because it will improve your work. Read it aloud to hear how it sounds. You are used to talking, and you often can "hear" that something is wrong when you cannot "see" it. Read your essay to a friend and ask him/her how it sounds.

Leave it a day before you re-write it. When you get too close to your own work, it's hard to see errors. Look for ways to improve the "flow" of your writing by making sure that one point leads logically to the next.

When you finish discussing a point, the next paragraph should relate to it. A simple way to do this is to write, "The first point is ..." and then "The second point is . . ." A more sophisticated way is to use the last sentence in your paragraph as a "connector" to the topic sentence in your next paragraph.

Using the example of Hitler, say your

paragraph ended with this sentence: "When the attempted revolt collapsed, Hitler was put on trial for treason." You begin your new paragraph with this sentence: "Hitler turned the trial into a public platform, making speeches which reached a wide audience." The word "trial" is your "connector" as it ends the one paragraph and begins the next.

What should you do if you cannot find a "connector"? Ask yourself two questions: "Why do I want to discuss this point next?" and "How does it fit in with what I want to say?" The answers should give you a first sentence in the new paragraph. It it doesn't, consider alternatives. Perhaps some other point logically comes next.

As you develop the major points in your writing, be sure to support your opinions with facts and logic. In some subjects everyone knows and accepts the facts. We all know that $2 + 2 = 4$. But if you write about why the U.S. lost the war in Vietnam, you're working with opinions and interpretations of the facts. You cannot say, "Everyone knows . . ." because people do not agree why the U.S. lost. You must present facts, illustrations and opinions in a logical way so the reader can understand your interpretation of why the U.S. lost.

When you present facts and opinions, you may use quotations. Make sure the quote supports your point and use a limited number.

The reader is more interested in what you have learned and in how you apply the information than in what the author of another book said.

When you present your facts and opinions, the cubing technique may cause you to write short sentences. As you gain experience in writing, you will learn to write longer, more complex sentences. But there is nothing wrong with writing simply. Hemingway used that style very successfully. A simple style can present your views very effectively.

Your writing will be most effective when you stick to the set length of your essay or report. When it is too long, the reader may become bored. When it is too short, you may leave out essential details. To expand what you write, use the cubing questions. To compress it, ask yourself, "What is the essence of what I want to say?" If you don't know how long your essay is, count the words.

Equally important is how you present your work. Type or write clearly. Some adult writing looks like ancient Egyptian hieroglyphics! Leave a margin on the left side of the page for your Lecturer to comment. Check your spelling, punctuation and grammar. Remember you want the reader to pay attention to what you wrote and not to concentrate on correcting errors.

THE LAST WORD

Writing is easy when you know how. You learn how by writing. Think about what you want to say. Start by making a list. Use the cubing technique to expand your ideas into an outline. Use your notes to develop a set of major points and turn these into paragraphs which present the important facts, opinions, interpretations and theories. Re-write your essay or report at least once to improve the flow. Most important of all, remember that you can learn to write and you will improve with practice.

CHAPTER 5

PREPARING FOR THE BIG "E" - TESTS AND EXAMS

Do you worry about tests and exams? Do you get butterflies in your stomach? Friends tell you, "Don't worry, you'll pass." But you still worry. It's like being seasick. You can't help thinking about it.

Let's begin with a negative thought: you will worry no matter what you do. Everybody worries, but you can control it. You worry because learning and passing are important to you. You want good results. You want to remember enough to pass.

Do you realize you start to prepare for the big "Big E" the same day you begin your course? When you read your textbook, you use the preview, read and review method. You ask yourself questions about what you read and hear. You listen actively, take notes and review periodically. You use what you learn in completing assignments. Good study habits are a very important part of preparing for tests and exams.

You learn by doing. In the early weeks you feel uncertain about what it all means. It seems so new and you realize how little you do know. A student summed up this feeling when she said, "I wish I had known at the beginning what I now know at the end because I would have gained so much more from the course!" Understanding often comes near or at the end of a course, and you have to do a lot of hard work before you get there.

As you work, you wonder, "How much am I expected to know and am I learning the right things?" One way to check your progress is to look at past exam papers. You may know someone who has done the course, or old exams may be on file in the library. If they are available, look at one to check if you are learning the right things. Do the questions make sense to you? Can you think of things you could say to answer them?

If you do this, do not make the mistake of learning answers to last year's questions in the hope that they will be repeated. Your goal is to understand and apply what you learn. Prior exams serve only as guidelines.

If you think about the work you have done, you can make up questions to check your knowledge. One student who was worried about a final exam, made up his own questions and answered them. He showed his work to the Lecturer who was amazed. The student had independently thought of three questions which were on the final exam and one which would have been included if the Lecturer had thought of it! That student was well prepared.

"BUT WHAT IF . . . ?"

Checking your knowledge is a logical way to cope with fear. But fear is an emotion and it does not always respond to logic. President Roosevelt said about the great depression in 1933, "There is nothing to fear but fear itself." If he was right, what can you do to overcome your fear?

Drugs do not help. Alcohol, tranquilizers and other drugs may reduce fear, making you feel "better", but they also affect your work. They interfere with your ability to think, remember and solve problems. If you are taking a drug under medical supervision, talk to the Doctor about whether it will affect your work. You don't want to feel tired and sleepy on the day of your exam.

"O.K. I won't take drugs, but suppose I forget what I have learned?" This can and does happen, but you can deal with it. One student coped this way.

"My mind went blank. Panic! I knew I had to do something. I closed my eyes and imagined I was back in your class until I could see the room. Then I thought about you and the sound of your voice until I could hear you. I got you talking and then had you talk about adult development. Finally I had you talk about things which related to the first question. At that point, everything came flooding back. I remembered."

An alternative way of doing this is to start writing. Write whatever comes into your mind. If you can't think of anything to write, write your name over and over, or draw loops until you think of something to write. Just writing helps break down your mental block.

If you have a mental block and forget, DO SOMETHING. The worst thing you can do is to sit and worry because your panic will grow.

"But what if I really do not know?" You can prepare and still miss something important. If this happens, there are several things you can do. If there is a choice of questions, pick another one. That seems obvious, but some students try to answer questions when they don't know the answer.

If you must answer that question, leave it for now and come back to it later. You may remember something which will help you. Use what you do know and relate this to the question. Try to show that what you know is relevant and answers the question. The worst that can happen is that you will get it wrong. The examiner must read your answer and decide if it has some value. A bad answer is always better than no answer.

There was one student who could not answer a question in her philosophy exam. She therefore wrote, "The answer to this question is known only to God. " The Lecturer wrote on her paper, "A for God, F for you." It was a nice try.

MIDNIGHT OIL AND OTHER METHODS

There is no one method of reviewing that works for everyone. Ideally it is better to begin your review at least a week before the exam, but some people leave it until the night before and still pass. When you begin your review will depend on what else you have to do.

You will remember more if you organize the things you want to learn under headings. Organize information around the "big ideas" or important concepts. Break these ideas down into smaller details.

Let's use the example of Hitler from Chapter 4. You think there may be a question on your exam about Hitler coming to power in 1933. First you decide what are the six or seven really important things that you need to know so you can write about this issue. Next to each big idea you then organize the smaller bits of information, facts, etc. which will help you.

Big Idea	Details
Munich revolt a mistake	Hitler doubtful, but agrees to lead revolt. Army remains loyal to government. Treason trial becomes propaganda platform.

Do not include a lot of detailed information in your outline. Include key points and facts to help you organize what you want to remember. It gives you a framework on which to organize information.

When you take your exam, this outline will help you remember information and answer the question. If there is a question about Hitler, you can quickly remember the six or seven major points you learned. Jot them down on a piece of paper. Decide which one you will use to begin your answer. These contain the detailed information to help you organize and write your answer.

If you have multiple choice questions or short answer questions, this review technigue will also help. When you read the question, it will act as a trigger for your memory and you will remember the relevant fact or detail to answer it.

The key to remembering is ORGANIZA-TION. When you arrange what you learn into a pattern which makes sense to you, you can talk, write and answer questions about it. If you simply memorize information by rote, you will only be able to repeat what you learn. For example, "In 1492 Columbus sailed the ocean blue" does help you remember that date, but not much else. That is rote learning. Exams ask why he went exploring and what were the consequences of his voyage.

Most tests and exams try to find out if you understand and can use the information in new situation. For example, in a mathematics exam you are given new problems to solve not the ones you did in class. When you review, be sure you understand and can apply the information as well as remember it.

BIG "E" DAY

Big "E" day will hold fewer surprises because you have prepared for it. There are several things you can do on the day which will improve your results.

It sounds obvious, but READ the directions. You can make a silly mistake and lose

points by not understanding what you are supposed to do.

Plan your time. For example, if there are ten short-answer questions and you have one hour, spend six minutes answering each question. If you have to write four essays and you have three hours, spend 45 minutes writing each one. Having made a schedule of your time, stick to it! When your time is up, go on to the next question, even if you are not finished. Come back to finish it after you have answered all the other questions.

Divide your time into preparation, writing and review. If you have 45 minutes to write an essay, take five minutes to plan it, 35 minutes to write it and five minutes to review and revise what you have written. If you have six minutes to write, divide your time into 30 seconds, five minutes, and 30 seconds. This way you can think about what you want to say before you write. You will write better answers.

Remember there is no prize for being the first to finish. If someone finishes early and you are still working, assume that they do not know as much as you do. It may not be true, but you will feel better!

Planning your time is equally important when you answer multiple choice questions. In one way these tests are easier because the right

answer is there. You do not have to remember it, only recognize it. Recognizing the correct answer can present problems for a careless student. Consider these four answers to a typical multiple choice question.

    A. Wrong.
    B. Partially correct, but incomplete. Wrong.
    C. Wrong.
    D. Complete answer. Right.

    Careless students do not read all the answers before making a choice. They select "B" which is wrong since "D" is a more complete answer. Read all the alternative answers and decide which one is the best answer.

    Answer all the questions you know first. If you do not know or cannot decide, leave the question and go on to the next. When you answer the ones you know first, this builds your self-confidence. Then go back and answer the other questions. You know how much time is left and how quickly you have to work.

But what about multiple choice questions where you do not know the correct answer. Don't leave them blank. Guess intelligently.

Intelligent guessing is using the process of elimination to improve your chances. Read all the, answers and try to eliminate one or two as wrong answers. This will improve the odds. When you guess one out of four, the odds of being right are one in four. One out of two are better odds.

THE LAST WORD

When all is said and done, what do you want? You want to pass and you want the satisfaction of knowing that you have learned something. This occurs when you use effective study skills because your exam review is built on a firm foundation. You can control your worry by using the suggestions in this chapter. Organize information into major points with supporting information to help you remember. When you take the exam, read the directions and use your knowledge effectively.

FINAL LAST WORD

It's up to you now, but you always knew it was. You have finished reading about how to improve your study skills. Now put these ideas into practice.

When you return to study, life is full of jolts. There are too many things to do and not enough time to do them. Friends may encourage you, but someone is sure to ask: "You're going back to study? How old will you be when you finish?"

The answer is easy. "The same age I will be if I don't do it."

Take it one day at a time. You will worry less and do more. When you look ahead, focus on where you are going. Don't borrow trouble worrying about things in the future. Solve problems if and when they arise.

Believe in yourself and your ability. Study is 95% hard work and 5% ability. There are bumps in the road, but others have made it. You will too.

Besides you have an advantage. You have read ADULT LEARNERS SURVIVAL SKILLS and you know what to do.

ABOUT THE AUTHOR :

Bill Bittel has taught classes to help adults and adolescents develop their skills for more than ten years. He has been a teacher for more than twenty years and is currently a Lecturer in adult education. He has degrees from Haverford College and Columbia University in the U.S.A. and from Oxford University in the U.K. As he spent several years as a mature age student, he understands the problems which confront them. Readers who wish to contact him may write to the Centre for Human Resource Studies, S.A. College of Advanced Education, Holbrooks Road, Underdale, S.A. 5032, Australia.

ABOUT THE ILLUSTRATOR :

Judy Bittel was a mature age student at the Flinders University of South Australia where she obtained a degree in Visual Arts and English. She studied fine arts in the U.S.A. where she won several competitions. She is now a registered developmental educator working with the intellectually handicapped.